Copycat Recipes

Making PF Chang's, Panda Express & Pei Wei Most Popular Chinese Recipes at Home

Lina Chang

Copyrights
All rights reserved © 2019 by Lina Chang and The Cookbook Publisher. No part of this publication or the information in it may be quoted from or reproduced in any form by means such as printing, scanning, photocopying, or otherwise without prior written permission of the copyright holder.

Disclaimer and Terms of Use
This book is presented solely for motivational and informational purposes. The author and the publisher do not hold any responsibility for errors, omissions, or contrary interpretation of the subject matter herein. The recipes provided in this book are for informational purposes only and are not intended to provide dietary advice. A medical practitioner should be consulted before making any changes in diet. Additionally, recipes' cooking times may require adjustment depending on age and quality of appliances. Readers are strongly urged to take all precautions to ensure ingredients are fully cooked in order to avoid the dangers of foodborne illnesses. The recipes and suggestions provided in this book are solely the opinions of the author. The author and publisher do not take any responsibility for any consequences that may result due to following the instructions provided in this book

ISBN: 9781095685051

Printed in the United States

— THE —
COOKBOOK
PUBLISHER

www.thecookbookpublisher.com

CONTENTS

INTRODUCTION	1
APPETIZERS	3
CHICKEN	27
BEEF AND PORK	69
FISH & SEAFOOD	89
VEGETARIAN AND SIDE DISHES	97
DESSERTS	113
RECIPE INDEX	125
ALSO BY LINA CHANG	127
APPENDIX Cooking Conversion Charts	129

INTRODUCTION

Asian food has become a go-to choice for many people, and everyone seems to have their favorite dishes to order when visiting the best-known Asian restaurants. Here you will find some of the most popular and well-loved dishes from Panda Express, PF Chang's, Pei Wei and more. These copycat recipes will let you get the taste of these dishes in the comfort of your own home. The recipes in this compilation are tributes to the originals, yet change them up just a bit to make it easier to prepare them in your own kitchen. From appetizers and soups to entrees and desserts, you are sure to find your favorite among these pages—or maybe you will discover a new dish you like even more!

For the ingredients, you will find most of what is needed in the Asian food aisle of your supermarket or grocery store, for wontons or egg roll wrappers in the freezer Chinese food section, and in the fresh produces for vegetables and fruits. If you have an Asian or Chinese market in your area, that's even better as you will have more options for brands. For stir-fries, I recommend the use of a wok but a deep skillet will do just fine.

The best part about these restaurant-inspired recipes is that you can tweak them to fit your own personal tastes. The recipe may call for meat to be grilled, but you can always bake it or cook it up in a skillet instead. Prefer shrimp over chicken or beef, just replace with your favorite protein. Don't like a certain vegetable or the level of spice? Just change the relevant ingredients so that the meal will delight you and your family. Now you have the freedom to make your favorite restaurant menus your own, so be creative and bring a delicious bit of Asia to your home!

APPETIZERS

Panda Express's Chicken Potstickers

Potstickers are a traditional Asian appetizer, and this copycat recipe from Panda Express is a delicious rendition.

Yields 50 | Prep. time 40 minutes | Cooking time 30 minutes

Ingredients
½ cup + 2 tablespoons soy sauce, divided
1 tablespoon rice vinegar
3 tablespoons chives, divided
1 tablespoon sesame seeds
1 teaspoon sriracha hot sauce
1 pound ground pork
3 cloves garlic, minced
1 egg, beaten

1½ tablespoons sesame oil
1 tablespoon fresh ginger, minced
50 dumpling wrappers
1 cup vegetable oil, for frying
1 quart water

Directions
1. In a mixing bowl, whisk together the ½ cup of soy sauce, vinegar, 1 tablespoon of the chives, sesame seeds and sriracha to make the dipping sauce.
2. In a separate bowl, mix together the pork, garlic, egg, the rest of the chives, the 2 tablespoons of soy sauce, sesame oil and the ginger.
3. Add about 1 tablespoon of the filling to each dumpling wrapper.
4. Pinch the sides of the wrappers together to seal. You may need to wet the edges a bit so they'll stick.
5. Heat the cup of oil in a large skillet. When hot, working in batches, add the dumplings and cook until golden brown on all sides. Take care of not overloading your pan.
6. Add the water and cook until tender, then serve with the dipping sauce.

Panda Express's Cream Cheese Rangoon

These delicious cheese-filled crispy bites are derived from the Panda Express recipe.

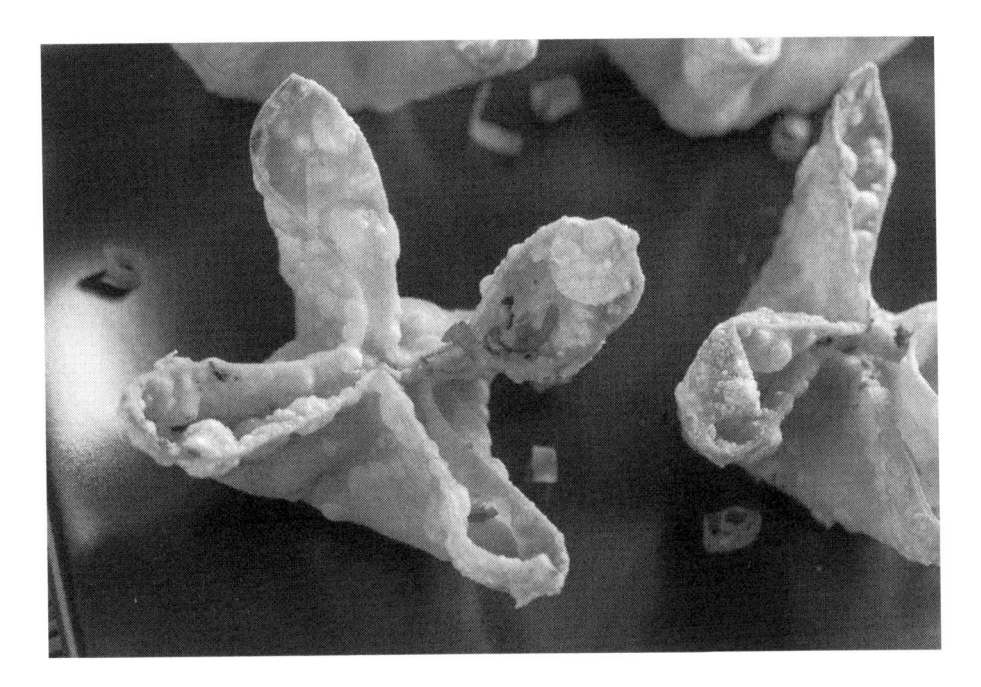

Makes 24 | Prep. time 5 minutes | Cooking time 5 minutes

Ingredients
¼ cup green onions, chopped
½ pound cream cheese, softened
½ teaspoon garlic powder
½ teaspoon salt
24 wonton wrappers
Oil for frying

Directions

1. Add the green onions, cream cheese, garlic powder and salt to a medium sized bowl and mix together.
2. Lay the wonton wrappers out and moisten the edges of the first one. Add about ½ tablespoon of filling to the center of the wrapper and seal by pinching the edges together, starting with the corners and working your way inward. Make sure it is sealed tightly. Repeat with the remaining wrappers.
3. Add about 3 inches of oil to a large pot. Heat it to about 350°F, then add the wontons a few at a time and cook until brown.
4. Remove from oil and place on a paper-towel-lined plate to drain.

Panda Express's Chicken Egg Roll

This Panda Express copycat recipe for chicken egg rolls will definitely excite your taste buds.

Serves 6–8 | Prep. time 10 minutes | Cooking time 5 minutes

Ingredients
2 tablespoons soy sauce, divided
2 cloves garlic, minced, divided
2 green onions, chopped, divided
3 tablespoons vegetable oil, divided
½ pound boneless skinless chicken breasts, cooked whole & cut in pieces
½ head green cabbage, thinly shredded
1 large carrot, peeled and shredded
1 cup bean sprouts
12–16 egg roll wrappers
1 tablespoon cornstarch mixed with 3 tablespoons water
Peanut Oil for frying

Directions
1. In a resealable plastic bag, combine 1 tablespoon of the soy sauce with 1 clove of minced garlic, 1 green onion, and 1 tablespoon of the oil. Mix well. Add the cut-up chicken pieces, seal the bag, and squish it around to make sure the chicken is covered. Refrigerate for at least 30 minutes.
2. After the chicken has marinated, pour 1 tablespoon of the oil into a large skillet and heat over medium-high heat. When the oil is hot, add the chicken and cook, stirring occasionally, until the chicken is cooked through.
3. Remove the chicken from the skillet and set aside. Pour the remaining tablespoon of oil into the skillet and add the cabbage, carrots and remaining soy sauce. Cook and stir until the carrots and cabbage start to soften, then add the bean sprouts and the remaining garlic and green onions. Cook another minute or so.
4. Drain the chicken and vegetables thoroughly using either a cheesecloth or a mesh strainer. Getting all the excess liquid out will keep the egg rolls from getting soggy.
5. In a large saucepan or Dutch oven, heat 3 inches of oil to 375°F.
6. Place about 2 tablespoons of the chicken and vegetables into the center of each egg roll wrapper. Fold the ends up and roll up to cover the filling. Seal by dipping your finger in the water and cornstarch mixture and covering the edges.
7. Cook the egg rolls in batches, a few at a time, for about five minutes or until golden brown and crispy. Remove from oil to a paper-towel-lined plate to drain.

Panda Express's Veggie Spring Roll

This Panda Express copycat recipe is great to as an appetizer—or take a couple to work for your lunch.

Serves 6–8 | Prep. time 15 minutes | Cooking time 5 minutes

Ingredients
4 teaspoons vegetable oil, divided
3 eggs, beaten
1 medium head cabbage, finely shredded
½ carrot, julienned
1 (8-ounce) can shredded bamboo shoots
1 cup dried, shredded wood ear mushroom, rehydrated
1 pound Chinese barbecue or roasted pork, cut into matchsticks
½ cup chopped Chinese yellow chives
1 green onion, thinly sliced
2½ teaspoons soy sauce
1 teaspoon salt

1 teaspoon sugar
1 (14-ounce) package egg roll wrappers
1 egg white, beaten
1 quart oil for frying, or as needed

Directions

1. In a large skillet, heat 1 tablespoon of oil over medium-high heat.
2. When the skillet is hot, add the beaten eggs and cook until firm, then flip and cook a bit longer like an omelet. When set, remove from the pan. Cut into strips and set aside.
3. Add the remaining oil to the skillet and heat. When hot, add the cabbage and carrot and cook for a couple of minutes until they start to soften. Then add the bamboo shoots, mushrooms, pork, green onions, chives, soy sauce, salt and sugar. Cook until the veggies are soft, then stir in the egg. Transfer the mixture to a bowl and refrigerate for about 1 hour.
4. When cooled, add about 2–3 tablespoons of filling to each egg roll wrapper. Brush some of the beaten egg around the edges of the wrapper and roll up, tucking in the ends first.
5. When all of the wrappers are filled, heat about 6 inches of oil to 350°F in a deep saucepan, Dutch oven or fryer.
6. Add the egg rolls to the hot oil a couple at a time. When golden brown and crispy, remove from oil to a paper-towel-lined plate to drain.
7. Serve with chili sauce or sweet and sour sauce.

PF Chang's Hot and Sour Soup

This hot and sour soup recipe pays tribute to the original you will find at PF Chang's.

Serves 4–6 | Prep. time 10 minutes | Cooking time 10 minutes

Ingredients
6 ounces chicken breasts, cut into thin strips
1 quart chicken stock
1 cup soy sauce
1 teaspoon white pepper
1 (6 ounce) can bamboo shoots, cut into strips
6 ounces wood ear mushrooms, cut into strips or canned straw mushrooms, if wood ear can't be found
½ cup cornstarch
½ cup water
2 eggs, beaten
½ cup white vinegar
6 ounces silken tofu, cut into strips
Sliced green onions for garnish

Directions
1. Cook the chicken strips in a hot skillet until cooked through. Set aside.
2. Add the chicken stock, soy sauce, pepper and bamboo shoots to a stockpot and bring to a boil. Stir in the chicken and let cook for about 3–4 minutes.
3. In a small dish, make a slurry with the cornstarch and water. Add a bit at a time to the stockpot until the broth thickens to your desired consistency.
4. Stir in the beaten eggs and cook for about 45 seconds or until the eggs are done.
5. Remove from the heat and add the vinegar and tofu.
6. Garnish with sliced green onions.

PF Chang's Lettuce Wraps

This is probably one of the most beloved appetizers on PF Chang's menu. This copycat recipe lets you make them at home any time you get the craving.

Serves 4 | Prep. time 10 minutes | Cooking time 10 minutes

Ingredients
1 tablespoon olive oil
1 pound ground chicken
2 cloves garlic, minced
1 onion, diced
¼ cup hoisin sauce
2 tablespoons soy sauce
1 tablespoon rice wine vinegar

1 tablespoon ginger, freshly grated
1 tablespoon Sriracha (optional)
1 (8-ounce) can whole water chestnuts, drained and diced
2 green onions, thinly sliced
Kosher salt and freshly ground black pepper to taste
1 head iceberg lettuce

Directions

1. Add the oil to a deep skillet or saucepan and heat over medium-high heat. When hot, add the chicken and cook until it is completely cooked through. Stir while cooking to make sure it is properly crumbled.
2. Drain any excess fat from the skillet, then add the garlic, onion, hoisin sauce, soy sauce, ginger, sriracha and vinegar. Cook until the onions have softened, then stir in the water chestnuts and green onion and cook for another minute or so. Add salt and pepper to taste.
3. Serve with lettuce leaves and eat by wrapping them up like a taco.

PF Chang's Shrimp Dumplings

This recipe was inspired by the amazing shrimp dumplings served at PF Chang's.

Serves 4–6 | Prep. time 20 minutes | Cooking time 10 minutes

Ingredients
1 pound medium shrimp, peeled, deveined, washed and dried , divided
2 tablespoons carrot, finely minced
2 tablespoons green onion, finely minced
1 teaspoon ginger, freshly minced
2 tablespoons oyster sauce
¼ teaspoon sesame oil
1 package wonton wrappers

Sauce

1 cup soy sauce
2 tablespoons white vinegar
½ teaspoon chili paste
2 tablespoons granulated sugar
½ teaspoon ginger, freshly minced
Sesame oil to taste
1 cup water
1 tablespoon cilantro leaves

Directions

1. In a food processor or blender, finely mince ½ pound of the shrimp.
2. Dice the other ½ pound of shrimp.
3. In a mixing bowl, combine both the minced and diced shrimp with the remaining ingredients.
4. Spoon about 1 teaspoon of the mixture into each wonton wrapper. Wet the edges of the wrapper with your finger, then fold up and seal tightly.
5. Cover and refrigerate for at least an hour.
6. In a medium bowl, combine all of the ingredients for the sauce and stir until well combined.
7. When ready to serve, boil water in a saucepan and cover with a steamer. You may want to lightly oil the steamer to keep the dumplings from sticking. Steam the dumplings for 7–10 minutes.
8. Serve with sauce.

PF Chang's Spicy Chicken Noodle Soup

Craving some PF Chang's spicy chicken soup? With this restaurant-inspired recipe you can make an excellent facsimile at home.

Serves 4–6 | Prep. time 15 minutes | Cooking time 15 minutes

Ingredients

2 quarts chicken stock
1 tablespoon granulated sugar
3 tablespoons white vinegar
2 cloves garlic, minced
1 tablespoon ginger, freshly minced
¼ cup soy sauce
Sriracha sauce to taste
Red pepper flakes to taste
1 pound boneless chicken breast, cut into thin 2–3 inch pieces
3 tablespoons cornstarch
Salt to taste
1 cup mushrooms, sliced
1 cup grape tomatoes, halved
3 green onions, sliced
2 tablespoons fresh cilantro, chopped
½ pound pasta, cooked to just under package directions and drained

Directions

1. Add the chicken stock, sugar, vinegar, garlic, ginger, soy sauce, Sriracha and red pepper flakes to a large saucepan. Bring to a boil, then lower the heat to a simmer. Let cook for 5 minutes.
2. Season chicken with salt to taste. In a resealable bag, combine the chicken and the cornstarch. Shake to coat.
3. Add the chicken to the simmering broth a piece at a time. Then add the mushrooms. Continue to cook for another 5 minutes.
4. Stir in the tomatoes, green onions, cilantro, and cooked pasta.
5. Serve with additional cilantro.

Takeout Dry Garlic Ribs

This rib recipe was inspired by all the wonderful Asian restaurants that serve this great appetizer.

Serves 4–6 | Prep. time 15 min | Cooking time 2 h and 30 min

Ingredients
6 pounds pork ribs, silver skin removed and cut into individual ribs
1½ cups broth

1½ cups brown sugar
¼ cup soy sauce
12 cloves garlic, minced
¼ cup yellow mustard
1 large onion, finely chopped
¼ teaspoon salt
½ teaspoon black pepper

Directions
1. Preheat oven to 200°F.
2. Season ribs with salt and pepper and place on a baking tray. Cover with aluminum foil and bake for 1 hour.
3. In a mixing bowl, stir together the broth, brown sugar, soy sauce, garlic, mustard and onion. Continue stirring until the sugar is completely dissolved.
4. After an hour, remove the foil from the ribs and turn the heat up to 350°F.
5. Carefully pour the sauce over the ribs. Re-cover with the foil and return to the oven for 1 hour.
6. Remove the foil and bake for 15 more minutes on each side.

Pei Wei's Thai Chicken Satay

These chicken satay sticks are a delicious take on the recipe offered at Pei Wei.

Serves 2–4 | Prep. time 20 minutes | Marinating time 4 hours | Cooking time 10–20 minutes

Ingredients
1 pound boneless, skinless chicken thighs
6-inch bamboo skewers, soaked in water

Thai satay marinade
1 tablespoon coriander seeds
1 teaspoon cumin seeds
2 teaspoons chopped lemongrass
1 teaspoon salt
1 teaspoon turmeric powder
¼ teaspoon roasted chili
½ cup coconut milk
1½ tablespoons light brown sugar
1 teaspoon lime juice
2 teaspoons fish sauce

Peanut sauce
2 tablespoons soy sauce
1 tablespoon rice wine vinegar
2 tablespoons brown sugar
¼ cup peanut butter
1 teaspoon chipotle Tabasco
Whisk all ingredients until well incorporated. Store in an airtight container in the refrigerator. Will last for 3 days.

Thai sweet cucumber relish
¼ cup white vinegar
¾ cup sugar
¾ cup water
1 tablespoon ginger, minced
1 Thai red chili, minced
1 medium cucumber
1 tablespoon toasted peanuts, chopped

Directions
1. Cut any excess fat from the chicken, then cut into strips about 3 inches long and 1 inch wide. Thread the strips onto the skewers.
2. Prepare the Thai Satay Marinade and the Peanut Sauce in separate bowls by simply whisking together all of the ingredients for each.
3. Dip the chicken skewers in the Thai Satay Marinade and allow to marinate for at least 4 hours. Reserve the marinade when you remove the chicken skewers.
4. You can either cook the skewers on the grill, basting with the marinade halfway through, or you can do the same in a 350 degree F oven. They taste better on the grill.
5. To prepare the Cucumber Relish, simply add all of the ingredients together and stir to make sure the cucumber is coated.
6. When the chicken skewers are done cooking, serve with peanut sauce and the cucumber relish.

Pei Wei's Vietnamese Chicken Salad Spring Roll

The chicken salad spring roll is a Pei Wei favorite, and this recipe is inspired by their delicious appetizer.

Serves 4–6 | Prep. time 10 minutes | Cooking time 1 minute

Ingredients
Salad
Rice Wrappers
Green leaf lettuce like Boston Bibb lettuce
Napa cabbage, shredded
Green onions, chopped
Mint, chopped
Carrots, cut into 1-inch matchsticks
Peanuts
Chicken, diced and cooked, about 6 chicken tenders drizzled with soy sauce, honey, garlic powder, and red pepper flakes

Lime dressing
2 tablespoons lime juice, about 1 lime
1½ teaspoons water
1 tablespoon sugar
1 teaspoon salt
Dash of pepper
3 tablespoons oil
Add everything but the oil to a small container or bowl and shake or stir until the sugar and salt are dissolved. Next, add the oil and shake well.

Peanut dipping sauce
2 tablespoons soy sauce
1 tablespoon rice wine vinegar
2 tablespoons brown sugar
¼ cup peanut butter
1 teaspoon chipotle Tabasco
1 teaspoon honey
1 teaspoon sweet chili sauce
1 teaspoon lime vinaigrette
Add all the ingredients to a small bowl and mix to combine thoroughly.

Directions
1. In a large bowl, mix together all of the salad ingredients except for the rice wrappers and lettuce.
2. Place the rice wrappers in warm water for about 1 minute to soften.
3. Transfer the wrappers to a plate and top each with 2 pieces of lettuce.
4. Top the lettuce with the salad mixture and drizzle with the lime dressing. Fold the wrapper by tucking in the ends and then rolling.
5. Serve with lime dressing and peanut dipping sauce.

Pei Wei's Crab Wonton

You can never have too many recipes for crab wonton, and this one was inspired by Pei Wei's brilliant recipe.

Serves 6 | Prep. time 10 minutes | Cooking time 5 minutes

Ingredients
1 (7-ounce) can white crab meat
½ pound cream cheese, softened
2–3 green onions, sliced
½ tablespoon garlic powder
Splash of soy sauce
Wonton wrappers
Cooking oil

Directions
1. Combine the crab, cream cheese, green onions, garlic powder and soy sauce in a bowl. Stir until the mixture reaches a paste-like consistency.
2. Spoon a bit of the mixture into each wonton wrapper and fold. Seal around the edges with a moistened finger.

CHICKEN

Panda Express's Grilled Teriyaki Chicken

This copycat teriyaki grilled chicken recipe allows you to experience the great taste of Panda Express at home.

Serves 4 | Prep. time 5 minutes | Cooking time 20 minutes

Ingredients
2 pounds chicken thighs
2 tablespoons canola oil
⅔ cup sugar
¼ cup low-sodium soy sauce
1 teaspoon lemon juice
½ teaspoon garlic powder
¼ teaspoon ground ginger
⅓ cup water
2 tablespoons cornstarch mixed with 2 tablespoons water
Sliced green onions for garnish

Directions
1. In a large bowl, combine the chicken thighs and canola oil and let sit until the grill is hot.
2. Place the chicken in a grill pan and grill for about 5 minutes on each side.
3. In a mixing bowl, combine the sugar, soy sauce, lemon juice, garlic powder, ground ginger and water. Heat to boiling, then reduce heat and simmer for 3 minutes. Stir in the cornstarch slurry and cook on low heat until the sauce thickens.
4. Spoon sauce over grilled chicken to serve. Sprinkle with sliced green onions.

Panda Express's Sweetfire Chicken Breast

A little spice mixed with a little sweetness is what makes this rendition of Panda Express sweetfire chicken so amazing.

Serves 4 | Prep. Time 15 minutes | Cooking time 15 minutes

Ingredients
3 large chicken breasts, cut into 1-inch pieces
1 (10-ounce) bottle sweet chili sauce
1 medium onion, sliced
1 large red bell pepper, chopped
1¼ cup pineapple chunks
¼ cup pineapple juice
2 cloves garlic, minced
1 cup all-purpose flour
2 eggs, beaten
Oil for frying
2 tablespoons oil, if needed
Salt and pepper to taste

Directions
1. Add the flour, salt and pepper to a shallow dish and mix well.
2. Dip the chicken pieces in the beaten egg followed by a dip in the flour to coat. Set aside.
3. Heat oil in a large skillet over medium-high heat. When hot, add the chicken pieces and cook until golden brown on all sides, about 6 minutes. You may have to work in batches, as you don't want the pieces to touch while cooking.
4. When done, remove the chicken from the skillet and place on a paper-towel-lined plate to drain excess oil.
5. If needed, add the rest of the oil to the skillet and heat over medium-high heat. When hot, add the onions, garlic and peppers and cook until the onions and peppers start to soften.
6. When soft, return the chicken to the skillet along with the chili sauce, pineapple and pineapple juice and allow to cook for about 7 minutes, stirring occasionally.
7. Serve with a side of rice.

Panda Express's Black Pepper Chicken

Black pepper chicken is a favorite among Panda Express diners.

Serves 4–6 | Prep. time 20 minutes | Cooking time 15 minutes

Ingredients
6 boneless, skinless chicken thighs
1 green bell pepper, diced
1 yellow onion, sliced
3 celery stalks, sliced
2 tablespoons cornstarch
1 tablespoon garlic powder
½ tablespoon black pepper
½ tablespoon onion powder
1 teaspoon ginger powder
2 tablespoons peanut oil
2 cups cooked rice

Sauce

½ cup chicken broth
¼ cup oyster sauce
¼ cup rice wine vinegar
½ tablespoon garlic, minced
1 teaspoon black pepper
1 teaspoon chili powder
½ teaspoon ginger powder

Directions
1. Combine all of the sauce ingredients, stir, and set aside.
2. Dice the chicken into 1-inch pieces.
3. Add the cornstarch, salt and pepper to a mixing bowl. Toss the chicken in the mixture to coat.
4. Heat the oil over medium-high heat in a large skillet.
5. Cook the chicken in batches to keep the pieces from touching. This lets the individual pieces cook faster and brown more easily.
6. When all of the chicken has been browned, return it to the skillet along with the vegetables and cook for about 5 more minutes.
7. Add the sauce to the chicken and vegetables and allow to simmer for 10–12 minutes.
8. Serve with rice.

Panda Express's
Zucchini Mushroom Chicken

Spiced just right, this luscious chicken is perfect for a one-pot meal.

Serves 4 | Prep. time 15 minutes | Cooking time 10 minutes

Ingredients
1 pound boneless skinless chicken breasts, cut into bite-sized pieces
3 tablespoons cornstarch
1 tablespoon canola oil
1 tablespoon sesame oil

½ pound mushrooms, sliced
1 medium zucchini, cut in half lengthwise, then into ½-inch slices
1 cup broccoli florets
¼ cup soy sauce
1 tablespoon rice wine vinegar
2 teaspoons sugar
3 cloves garlic, minced
2 teaspoons minced ginger or ½ teaspoon ground ginger
Sesame seeds, for garnish (optional)

Directions
1. Add the cornstarch to a shallow dish and season with salt and pepper. Add the chicken and toss to coat.
2. In a large skillet, heat both the canola and sesame oil over medium high-heat.
3. When hot, add the chicken and cook until brown on all sides.
4. Remove the chicken from the skillet and turn the heat to high.
5. Cook the zucchini, mushrooms, and broccoli until they begin to soften, about 1 minute.
6. Stir in the garlic and ginger and cook a bit longer. Continue to cook until the mushrooms and zucchini have softened to taste, then stir the chicken back into the skillet.
7. When the chicken has heated up, stir in the soy sauce and the rice wine vinegar.
8. Serve with rice.

Panda Express's Orange Chicken

So many people love the orange chicken from Panda Express. This copycat recipe lets you get those amazing flavors at home.

Serves 4–6 | Prep. Time 15 minutes | Cooking time 10 minutes

Ingredients
2 pounds boneless skinless chicken, chopped into bite-sized pieces
1 egg
1½ teaspoons salt
White pepper to taste
Oil for frying
½ cup cornstarch
¼ cup flour

Orange sauce
3 tablespoons soy sauce
¾ cup orange juice
½ cup brown sugar
Zest of 1 orange
1 tablespoon oil
2 tablespoons ginger, minced
2 teaspoons garlic, minced
1 teaspoon red chili flakes
½ cup green onion, chopped
2 tablespoons rice wine
½ cup water
2 tablespoons cornstarch
1 teaspoon sesame oil

Directions
1. In a shallow dish, combine the ½ cup of cornstarch and the flour.
2. In a second shallow dish, beat together the egg, salt, pepper and 1 tablespoon of oil.
3. In a large skillet or deep saucepan, heat oil to 375°F.
4. Dredge the chicken pieces in the egg mixture followed by the flour mixture. Shake off any excess flour. Add the coated chicken to the hot oil and cook for about 4 minutes or until nicely browned.
5. Transfer the chicken from the hot oil to a paper-towel-lined plate to drain.
6. In a mixing bowl, stir together the soy sauce, orange juice, brown sugar and orange zest.
7. In another skillet or wok, heat 1 tablespoon of oil. When hot, add the ginger, garlic, red pepper flakes and green onions. Cook for about 1 minute or until the garlic is fragrant.
8. Stir in the rice wine and soy sauce mixture. Cook for about 1 more minute, then add the chicken.
9. Make a slurry with the water and remaining cornstarch and gradually add to the skillet until the sauce thickens. Add sesame oil to taste.
10. Serve with rice.

PF Chang's Orange Peel Chicken

Although similar to the orange chicken at Panda Express, this orange peel chicken recipe inspired by that of PF Chang's is a bit spicier—but it's just as delicious!

Serves 4 | Prep. time 10 minutes | Cooking time 30 minutes

Ingredients
4 boneless, skinless chicken breasts
¾ cup flour
¼ cup orange peel from 1 orange
2 tablespoons cornstarch
2 tablespoons garlic, minced
2 teaspoons black pepper
2 teaspoons Creole seasoning
2 teaspoons garlic powder
2 teaspoons onion powder
1 teaspoon chili powder
Extra-virgin olive oil

Orange peel sauce
1 cup tomato sauce
6 tablespoons orange juice
6 tablespoons chicken broth
¼ cup brown sugar
2 tablespoons sriracha
1 tablespoon soy sauce
1 teaspoon chili paste
¼ teaspoon black pepper

Directions
1. Peel and clean an orange, removing the white pulpy part and cutting out the segments which will be used for garnish. Julienne the peel and set aside with the segments.
2. Stir together all of the sauce ingredients in a mixing bowl. Set aside.
3. Cut the chicken into bite-sized cubes. In another bowl, mix together all of the spices. Toss over the chicken pieces. Stir to make sure the chicken is properly covered.
4. In a small dish, stir together the flour and cornstarch. Pour over the seasoned chicken and stir again to make sure the chicken is coated.
5. Heat the olive oil in a large skillet over medium-high heat. When hot, stir in the chicken and cook until browned on all sides. You may have to work in batches to cook the chicken faster and more evenly.
6. When all the chicken has been cooked, remove it from the skillet.
7. Add a bit more olive oil to the pan, then toss in the orange peel slices and the garlic and cook just until garlic is fragrant.
8. Add the sauce to the skillet and bring to a boil, then reduce heat and cook for 5 minutes or until the sauce begins to thicken.
9. Return the chicken to the skillet and cook for 5 more minutes.
10. Garnish with orange segments and serve with rice

PF Chang's Chicken Fried Rice

Chicken fried rice is an Asian restaurant staple, and this take on the fried rice at PF Chang's is sure to please.

Serves 4 | Prep. time 10 minutes | Cooking time 10 minutes

Ingredients
2 cups prepared rice
1 chicken breast, cut into bite-sized pieces and seasoned with salt & pepper
½ cup frozen mixed vegetables
2 green onions, chopped
1 clove garlic, minced
1 egg
3 teaspoons sesame or wok oil, divided
2 tablespoons soy sauce

Directions
1. In a small dish, beat together the egg and 1 teaspoon of oil.
2. In a large skillet or wok, heat another teaspoon of the oil and cook the chicken until done. Remove from skillet and set aside.
3. Add the last teaspoon of oil to the skillet and stir in the mixed vegetables and green onions. Cook and stir until hot and tender. Then add the garlic and cook until fragrant.
4. Using a spatula or spoon, move the vegetables to one side. Add the egg mixture and scramble until cooked, then add the chicken and stir until it is all combined.

PF Chang's Ginger Chicken with Broccoli

This is a favorite dish from PF Chang's, and this copycat recipe is a fine tribute to the original.

Serves 4 | Prep. time 10 minutes | Cooking time 20 minutes

Ingredients
½ cup egg substitute or beaten eggs
¼ teaspoon white pepper
¼ teaspoon salt
1 pound boneless, skinless chicken breasts, sliced

Stir-fry sauce
½ cup soy sauce
2 tablespoons rice wine vinegar
1 tablespoon sugar
½ cup chicken broth
3 cups chicken broth

½ pound broccoli florets
2 tablespoons butter
2 tablespoons ginger, freshly minced
2 tablespoons green onion, minced
1 teaspoon garlic, minced
¼ cup cornstarch
1 teaspoon sesame oil

Directions
1. In a resealable bag, combine the eggs or egg substitute, salt and pepper. Add the chicken pieces and seal. Place in the refrigerator for at least 3 hours or overnight.
2. When ready to use, discard the marinade.
3. Stir together all of the ingredients for the stir-fry sauce in a mixing bowl. Mix well and set aside.
4. Add the 3 cups of chicken broth to a large skillet or wok and bring to a boil. Reduce heat to maintain a simmer. Add the chicken and cook until almost done, then remove from the pot.
5. Add the broccoli to the broth and cook until tender. Then drain the broth and transfer the broccoli to a plate.
6. Add the butter to the skillet and heat over medium heat. When melted, stir in the ginger, green onion and garlic and cook until the garlic is fragrant.
7. Return the to the skillet and cook until done, about 5 minutes.
8. Thicken the broth with a slurry made from the cornstarch and ½ cup of water. Cook until the sauce thickens.
9. Serve the chicken over rice and broccoli.

P.F. Chang's Crispy Honey Chicken

Nothing hits the spot quite like Asian honey chicken dishes. Make some of this dish right at home and enjoy the Asian comfort food.

Serves 4 | Prep. time 20 minutes | Cooking time 2 hours

Ingredients
Chicken
1 pound chicken breast, boneless, skinless, cut into medium sized chunks
Vegetable oil, for frying and deep frying

Batter
4 ounces all-purpose flour
2½ ounces cornstarch
1 egg
6 ounces water
⅛ teaspoon baking powder
⅛ teaspoon baking soda

<u>Chicken seasoning</u>
1 tablespoon light soy sauce
⅛ teaspoon white pepper
¼ teaspoon kosher salt
1 tablespoon cornstarch

<u>Sauce</u>
½ cup sake or rice wine
½ cup honey
3 ounces rice vinegar
3 tablespoons light soy sauce
6 tablespoons sugar
¼ cup cornstarch
¼ cup water

Preparation
1. Make the batter at least 2 hours in advance.
2. Mix all the batter ingredients together and refrigerate.
3. After an hour and 40 minutes, mix all the seasoning ingredients together and mix in the chicken. Make sure that the chicken is covered entirely.
4. Place the chicken in the refrigerator to marinate for at least 20 minutes.
5. Mix all the sauce ingredients together - except the cornstarch and water - and set aside.
6. Before you begin frying your chicken:
    a) Place a paper towel on a plate in preparation for draining the oil; and
    b) Heat your oil to 350°F.
7. When your oil is heated, remove the chicken from the refrigerator and pour the batter all over it.
8. One by one, lower the coated chicken pieces into the heated oil. Keep them suspended until the batter is cooked, about 20 to 30 seconds.

9. When all the chicken is cooked, place it on the plate covered with the paper towel to cool and drain.
10. Bring the sauce mixture to a boil. While waiting for it to boil, mix the cornstarch and water in a separate bowl.
11. Slowly pour the cornstarch mixture into the sauce and continue cooking for 2 minutes, until the sauce thickens.
12. When the sauce thickens, remove it from heat.
13. When the chicken is cooked, pour some sauce over the entire mixture, just enough to cover the chicken.
14. Transfer everything to a plate with rice or Chinese noodles and serve.

Pei Wei's Sesame Chicken

Sesame Chicken is another Asian restaurant favorite. This recipe inspired by the dish at Pei Wei is sure to please.

Serves 4–6 | Prep. time 20 minutes | Cooking time 15 minutes

Ingredients
Sauce
½ cup soy sauce
2½ tablespoons hoisin sauce
½ cup sugar
¼ cup white vinegar
2½ tablespoons rice wine
2½ tablespoons chicken broth

Pinch of white pepper
1¼ tablespoons orange zest

Breaded chicken
2 pounds boneless skinless chicken breasts
¼ cup cornstarch
½ cup flour
1 egg
2 cups milk
Pinch of white pepper
Pinch of salt
1 quart vegetable oil
½ red bell pepper, chunked
½ white onion, chunked
1 tablespoon Asian chili sauce
½ tablespoon ginger, minced
¼ cup scallions, white part only, cut into rings
1 tablespoon sesame oil
1 tablespoon cornstarch
1 tablespoon water
Sesame seeds for garnish

Directions
1. Prepare the sauce by whisking all of the ingredients together in a small saucepan. Bring to a simmer, then remove from the heat and set aside.
2. Whisk the eggs, milk, salt and pepper together in a shallow dish.
3. Mix the ¼ cup of cornstarch and flour together in a separate shallow dish.
4. Dredge the chicken pieces in the egg mixture and then in the cornstarch/flour mixture. Shake off any excess, then set aside.
5. Heat the vegetable oil over medium-high heat in a deep skillet or saucepan.

6. When hot, drop the coated chicken into the oil and cook for about 2–4 minutes. Remove from oil and place on a paper-towel-lined plate to drain.
7. Make a slurry out of the 1 tablespoon of cornstarch and water.
8. In a different large skillet or wok, heat 1 tablespoon of sesame oil until hot. Add the ginger and chili sauce and heat for about 10 seconds.
9. Add the peppers and onions and cook for another 30 seconds. Stir in the chili sauce and ginger and the sauce you made earlier and bring to a boil. Once it boils, stir in the cornstarch slurry and cook until the sauce thickens.
10. When the sauce is thick, add the chicken and stir to coat.
11. Serve with rice, and sprinkle with sesame seeds.

Pei Wei's Spicy Chicken

This spicy chicken recipe, which is derived from the classic dish served at Pei Wei, will satisfy your craving in the comfort of your own kitchen.

Serves 4 | Prep. time 10 minutes | Cooking time 15 minutes

Ingredients
2 boneless skinless chicken breasts, cut into 1-inch pieces
1½ cups sliced carrots
1½ cups sugar snap peas
3 cups vegetable oil for frying

Batter
1½ cups flour
1½ teaspoons salt
1½ teaspoons baking soda

2 eggs
⅔ cup milk
⅔ cup water

Sauce
3 teaspoons vegetable oil
3 tablespoons minced garlic
¼ cup green onion, chopped, white parts only
1½ cups pineapple juice
3 teaspoons chili garlic paste, more if you want it spicier
3 tablespoons white wine vinegar
2 tablespoons sugar
2 teaspoons soy sauce
1 teaspoon salt
4 teaspoons cornstarch
3 tablespoons water

Directions
1. In a mixing bowl, stir together all of the ingredients for the batter. It should be smooth and without lumps. It will be thinnish.
2. In a saucepan, bring 3 cups of water to a boil then add the carrots and peas and cook just until tender. You want them to be a bit crispy. Drain and set aside.
3. In a deep pot or deep fryer, heat the 3 cups of oil to 375°F. Add the chicken to the hot oil a few pieces at a time. Leave it there until cooked through and golden brown, then transfer to a paper-towel-lined plate to drain.
4. In a large skillet or wok, heat 2 teaspoons of oil over medium-high heat. Add the garlic and green onion and cook for about 1 minute.
5. In a bowl, stir together all of the sauce ingredients except for the cornstarch and water.
6. Add the sauce mixture to the hot skillet and cook until it starts to bubble. Make a slurry of the cornstarch and water and add it to the bubbling sauce, and cook until the sauce starts to thicken.
7. Add the chicken, peas and carrots and cook until hot.
8. Serve with rice.

Pei Wei's Chicken Pad Thai

Pei Wei is famous for their Pad Thai. This copycat recipe lets you make the delicious dish at home.

Serves 4–6 | Prep. time 15 minutes | Cooking time 15 minutes

Ingredients
½ cup low-fat coconut milk
6 tablespoons creamy peanut butter
¼ cup light soy sauce
¼ cup lime juice

½ tablespoon rice wine vinegar
2 tablespoons brown sugar
2 teaspoons grated ginger
½ teaspoon red pepper flakes

Chicken stir-fry
½ tablespoon canola oil
½ tablespoon dark sesame oil
1–2 teaspoons curry powder (optional)
1 pound chicken breast, cut into bite-sized pieces
6–8 ounces frozen sugar snap peas
1 medium onion, chopped
2 cloves garlic, minced
½ pound cooked rice noodles or long thin pasta

Garnish
¼ cup lightly salted dry roasted peanuts, chopped
Cilantro

Directions
1. Stir together all of the sauce ingredients in a mixing bowl. Combine well, then set aside.
2. Cook the noodles or pasta according to the package directions. Set aside.
3. Heat the canola oil and sesame oil in a large skillet over medium-high heat. When hot, add the chicken and stir. Allow to cook for about 5 minutes, then stir in the garlic.
4. When the chicken is completely cooked through, add the peas and cook a bit longer to heat the peas through.
5. Stir in the sauce and make sure the chicken is evenly coated.
6. Add the cooked noodles and stir to make sure everything is covered in the sauce.
7. Serve with cilantro and top with chopped peanuts.

Pei Wei's Kung Pao Chicken

One of the favorite dishes on the Pei Wei menu, this Kung Pao chicken is easy to make at home and can be adjusted to the spice level you like.

Serves 4–6 | Prep. time 15 minutes | Cooking time 10 minutes

Ingredients

Sauce
1 teaspoon red chili paste
2 tablespoons low-sodium soy sauce
1 tablespoon mirin
1 teaspoon seasoned rice wine vinegar
1 teaspoon sugar
¼ cup chicken broth
1 teaspoon cornstarch
1 teaspoon dark sesame oil

Stir-fry
1½ pounds boneless, skinless chicken breasts, cut into 1-inch cubes
1 egg, whisked
¼ cup cornstarch
¼ cup canola oil
½ cup frozen crinkle-cut carrots
1 cup sugar snap peas
½ cup dry-roasted peanuts
10 dried red chili peppers, if you want a bit more spice you can also add a dash of red pepper flakes
4 green onions, including green parts, sliced
3 cloves garlic, minced
½ cup water chestnuts, diced

Directions

1. Beat the egg in a small shallow dish. Add the cornstarch to another shallow dish.
2. Mix together all the ingredients for the sauce in a small bowl and set aside.
3. Bread the chicken by first dipping in the egg and then coating with cornstarch.
4. Heat the oil over medium-high heat in a large skillet or a wok. When hot, add the coated chicken. Cook through and brown on all sides, then remove chicken to a paper-towel-lined plate to drain.
5. Add a bit more oil to the same skillet and heat. When hot, add the peas, chestnuts, and carrots. Cook for 1–2 minutes. Remove the vegetables from the skillet and place them on top of the chicken.
6. Add a bit more oil to the skillet, if needed, and quickly sauté the peanuts and chili peppers. They only need to cook for a short time. Add them to the plate with the chicken and vegetables when they are done.
7. Add the green onions, and garlic to the skillet and cook just until fragrant, about 1 minute.
8. Return everything else to the skillet, then add the sauce and stir to make sure everything is coated. Cook until the sauce starts to thicken.
9. Serve with rice.

Pei Wei's Chicken Lo Mein

This Chicken Lo Mein recipe is once again inspired by the menu item of the same name from Pei Wei.

Serves 4 | Prep. time 15 minutes | Cooking time 30 minutes

Ingredients
1½ pounds boneless, skinless chicken breast, sliced very thinly

Marinade
1 tablespoon soy sauce
1½ teaspoons cornstarch
2 tablespoons oyster sauce
2 teaspoons soy sauce
¼ cup beef broth
1 tablespoon sugar

Other ingredients
6 ounces linguine, cooked
1 teaspoon sesame oil
¼ cup oil
1 clove garlic, chopped
1 carrot, chopped into ½-inch pieces
½ cup cabbage, chopped
1 cup mushrooms, sliced
1 cup bean sprouts
3 green onions, both green and white parts, sliced

Directions
1. Combine all of the ingredients for the marinade in a resealable bag. Add the chicken pieces and refrigerate for at least 20 minutes.
2. In a small mixing bowl, stir together the oyster sauce, soy sauce, beef broth and sugar.
3. Toss the cooked noodles with the sesame oil.
4. Add the ¼ cup of oil to a large skillet or wok and heat over medium-high heat.
5. Add the chicken, reserve the marinade, and cook for about 5 minutes or until cooked through. Remove from the skillet and set aside.
6. Add another tablespoon of oil to the skillet if you need to. When the oil is hot, add the garlic and sauté until fragrant, then add the carrots.
7. Cook for 1 minute. Add the cabbage and mushrooms and cook for about 2 more minutes. Stir the cooked noodles into the pan and cook for another 2 minutes.
8. Add the marinade from the resealable bag along with the cooked chicken. Allow to cook for another 3–5 minutes, then serve with rice.

Pei Wei's Thai Blazing Noodles with Chicken

This spicy noodle recipe is a take on the Blazing Noodles you can find at Pei Wei.

Serves 4 | Prep. time 10 minutes | Cooking time 10 minutes

Ingredients
¾ cup soy sauce
6 tablespoons mushroom oyster sauce
¼ cup sriracha sauce
6 tablespoons ketchup
4 teaspoons rice vinegar
1 teaspoon black pepper

Chicken
2 pounds boneless skinless chicken breasts, cut into bite-sized pieces

Cornstarch
1 egg
2 cups milk
¼ teaspoon white pepper
⅛ teaspoon salt

Noodles
2 (12-ounce) packages refrigerated Chow Fun noodles
1 tablespoon vegetable oil
½ cup carrot, sliced
½ cup snap peas
⅓ cup green onion, tops only
⅓ cup Thai basil
1 tablespoon cilantro leaf
½ cup tomatoes, chopped
1 tablespoon garlic, minced
Crushed peanuts for garnish

Directions
1. In a mixing bowl, whisk together the soy sauce, oyster sauce, sriracha, ketchup, vinegar and pepper. Set aside.
2. In a shallow dish, beat together the eggs, milk, salt and pepper.
3. Place the cornstarch into another shallow dish.
4. Dredge the chicken pieces first in the egg mixture and then in the cornstarch. Shake off any excess.
5. In a large saucepan, bring 2 quarts of water to a boil. Add the chicken and cook for 4 minutes, then remove to a paper-towel-lined plate.
6. In a large skillet or wok, heat 1 tablespoon of vegetable oil over high heat. When it starts to smoke, add the garlic and tomatoes. Let cook for 30 seconds, then add the chicken and cook for another 10 seconds.
7. Add the noodles, peas and carrots. Let cook for a minute or so, then add the sauce you prepared earlier. Stir until the sauce is evenly distributed.
8. Add the green onions, basil and cilantro and sprinkle with crushed peanuts before serving.

Pei Wei's Honey Seared Chicken

This deliciously sweet and salty recipe is inspired by Pei Wei's honey seared chicken.

Serves 4 | Prep. time 2 hours 30 minutes | Cooking time 25 minutes

Ingredients
Batter
1 cup flour
⅔ cup cornstarch
1 egg
¾ cup water
⅛ teaspoon baking soda
⅛ teaspoon baking powder

Chicken
1 pound boneless chicken breast, cut into bite-sized pieces
1 tablespoon soy sauce
⅛ teaspoon white pepper
¼ teaspoon kosher salt
1 tablespoon cornstarch
1 tablespoon chives or green onions, sliced thin, for garnish

Sauce:
½ cup sake or rice wine
½ cup honey
3 ounces rice vinegar
3 tablespoons soy sauce
6 tablespoons sugar
¼ cup cornstarch

Directions

1. Combine all of the batter ingredients in a mixing bowl. Stir to combine completely, then refrigerate for at least 2 hours.
2. Coat the chicken pieces with all of the seasoning ingredients. Refrigerate for at least 20 minutes.
3. Heat about 2 cups of oil in a deep skillet or saucepan. Coat the seasoned chicken pieces with the batter and add them to the oil. Cook for about 4–5 minutes or until the chicken is cooked through and golden brown.
4. Combine all of the sauce ingredients except for the cornstarch in a saucepan. In a separate bowl, mix the cornstarch with ¼ cup of water. Bring the sauce to a boil and then slowly whisk in the cornstarch slurry. Boil for another couple of minutes until the sauce thickens to a honey-like consistency.
5. Serve warm with rice or noodles and garnish with chiseled chives or sliced green onions.

Pei Wei's Coconut Curry with Chicken

Pei Wei's Coconut Curry is delicious. This recipe is pretty close to the awe-inspiring original.

Serves 4–6 | Prep. time 5 minutes | Cooking time 20 minutes

Ingredients

Meat from one whole chicken, or 6–8 chicken tenderloins, cooked
1 cup snow pea pods
2 red bell peppers, chopped
1 yellow or white onion, chopped
3 carrots, chopped
5 cloves garlic, minced
1-inch piece of ginger, minced
2 (14-ounce) cans full-fat coconut milk
½ (2.8-ounce) pouch green curry paste
One bunch Thai basil or regular basil, roughly chopped
Salt and pepper to taste

Directions

1. Whisk together the coconut milk and green curry paste in a medium saucepan. Bring to a simmer.
2. Add the cooked chicken and all of the vegetables. Continue to simmer until the vegetables are cooked through to your desired softness, about 15–20 minutes.
3. Serve with rice.

Pei Wei's Chopped Chicken Salad

A deliciously light and refreshing salad is always a great choice, and this recipe is no exception. Inspired by Pei Wei's chopped chicken salad, you will love this dish as a side salad or a meal in and of itself.

Serves 2–4 | Prep. time 15 minutes | Cooking time 0

Ingredients
1 (10.5-ounce) package Chopped Asian Salad Mix, without dressing
2 baby bok choy, chopped
1 cup grape tomatoes, chopped
2 cups cooked chicken, shredded
¼ cup green onions
Sesame seeds for garnish

Dressing

6 tablespoons rice vinegar
3 teaspoons fresh ginger
2 cloves garlic, grated or finely minced
1 tablespoon agave nectar or honey
3 teaspoons Chinese five-spice
1 tablespoon green onion, minced
Salt and pepper to taste

Directions
1. Whisk together all of the dressing ingredients in a small bowl.
2. Mix together all of the salad ingredients in a salad bowl.
3. Toss the dressing onto the salad or serve on the side.
4. Garnish with sesame seeds.

Pei Wei's Asian Diner Carame

This caramel chicken recipe is inspired by the a served at Pei Wei.

Serves 6 | Prep. time 20 minutes | Cooking time 55 minutes

Ingredients

1 cup sugar
¼ cup water
¾ cup reduced-sodium chicken broth

...ons fish sauce
...spoons soy sauce
...ole chicken, cut in 10 pieces
1 teaspoon salt
2 tablespoons vegetable oil and more, if needed
¼ cup fresh ginger, chopped
2 tablespoons fresh garlic, chopped
½ large red onion, chopped
2 tablespoons jalapenos, chopped
1 English cucumber, sliced then julienned
½ red bell pepper, julienned lengthwise
1 carrot, cut diagonally
2 green onions, chopped
½ cup pineapple chunks
¼ cup fresh mint, chopped
¼ cup fresh cilantro, chopped
¼ cup fresh basil, chopped
Cooked rice or rice vermicelli for serving

Vietnamese vinaigrette
½ cup lime juice, plus wedges for serving
¼ cup light brown sugar
2 tablespoons Vietnamese fish sauce
½ teaspoon toasted sesame oil
4 teaspoons vegetable oil

Directions
1. Preheat oven to 325°F.
2. Combine sugar and water in a deep sauce pot. Bring to a boil and simmer until the sugar turns a dark caramel color. Do not let it burn, and do not stir the sugar while cooking or it may crystallize.
3. Add the chicken broth. The broth will boil quickly and spatter because of the hot sugar, so be careful! This is the reason for the deep pot.

4. Stir in the broth and continue stirring over low heat until the sugar dissolves. Add the fish sauce and soy sauce. Set aside.
5. Combine the Vietnamese vinaigrette ingredients in a medium bowl and add cucumbers, red bell peppers and carrots. Marinate until ready to use.
6. Season the chicken pieces with the salt.
7. Heat the vegetable oil in a large Dutch oven and brown the chicken pieces on all sides. Set aside.
8. In the same pan, using the extra vegetable oil if needed, sauté the ginger, garlic, red onion and jalapeno over medium heat for 4–5 minutes until soft and fragrant.
9. Add the browned chicken pieces and the caramel sauce to the Dutch oven, turning the chicken in the caramel broth to coat all sides. Arrange the chicken so it is all submerged in the sauce as much as possible and bring to a boil.
10. Cover the pot, put in the oven and braise until done, about 35–45 minutes. While the chicken is cooking, assemble the green onion, pineapple chunks and the other herbs and set aside.
11. Just before serving, add the green onions and pineapple chunks and stir well. Serve the chicken over rice or rice vermicelli. Top with a portion of Vietnamese vinaigrette slaw.

BEEF AND PORK

Panda Express's Beijing Beef

This recipe with crispy strips of beef and a little bit of spice is a tasty tribute to the dish served at Panda Express.

Serves 4 | Prep. time 20 minutes | Cooking time 15 minutes

Ingredients
1 pound flank steak
1 cup canola oil

4 cloves garlic, minced
1 yellow onion, sliced
1 red bell pepper, cut into 1-inch strips
2 tablespoons + 1 teaspoon cornstarch, divided
¼ teaspoon salt
3 egg whites, beaten
½ cup water
¼ cup sugar
3 tablespoons ketchup
6 tablespoons hoisin sauce
1 tablespoon soy sauce
2 teaspoons oyster sauce
4 teaspoons sweet chili sauce
1 teaspoons crushed red peppers
2 tablespoons apple cider vinegar

Directions
1. Cut the flank steak against the grain into ¼-inch slices.
2. Place the beef, egg, salt and 1 teaspoon of cornstarch in a mixing bowl. Cover and refrigerate for at least an hour.
3. In another mixing bowl, whisk together the water, sugar, ketchup, hoisin sauce, soy sauce, oyster sauce, chili sauce, crushed red pepper and apple cider vinegar.
4. Remove the beef from the refrigerator and place it in a separate dish. Discard the remaining marinade. Sprinkle the beef with 2 tablespoons of cornstarch and stir. Shake off any excess cornstarch.
5. In a medium saucepan, heat the oil over medium-high heat. When hot, fry the beef in batches, about 2–3 minutes. Remove from oil and set on a paper-towel-lined plate to drain.
6. To a large skillet, add 2 tablespoons of the same oil you fried the beef in. Heat over medium-high heat. When hot, add the onion and pepper and cook for about 3 minutes.
7. Add the garlic and cook about 30 seconds more, then remove from the skillet and add to the plate with the beef.
8. Add the sauce you prepared earlier to the skillet and cook over high heat until it thickens. Add the beef and vegetables, stirring to coat.

Panda Express's Copycat Beef and Broccoli

Who doesn't love Panda Express? Whip up this quick and delicious copycat go-to stir-fry in just 45 minutes.

Serves 4 | Prep. time 30 minutes | Cooking time 15 minutes

Ingredients
2 tablespoons cornstarch, divided
3 tablespoons Chinese rice wine, divided
1 pound flank steak, cut thinly against the grain
1 pound broccoli florets, chopped into small pieces
2 tablespoons oyster sauce
2 tablespoons water
1 tablespoon brown sugar
1 tablespoon soy sauce
1 tablespoon cornstarch
2 tablespoons canola oil
¼ teaspoon sesame oil

1 teaspoon ginger, finely chopped
2 cloves garlic, finely chopped
2 teaspoons sesame seeds

Preparation

1. In a large Ziploc bag, add 1 tablespoon cornstarch and 2 tablespoons Chinese rice wine. Place beef inside and seal tightly. Massage bag to fully coat beef. Set aside to marinate for at least 20 minutes.
2. Rinse broccoli and place in a nonreactive bowl. Place a wet paper towel on top, then microwave for 2 minutes. Set aside.
3. Stir oyster sauce, water, 1 tablespoon Chinese rice wine, brown sugar, soy sauce, and remaining cornstarch in a bowl until well mixed. Set aside.
4. Heat wok over high heat. You want the wok to be very hot. Then, heat canola and sesame oil in wok and wait to become hot.
5. Working in batches, add steak and cook over high heat for 1 minute. Flip, and cook other side for another 1 minute. Transfer to a plate.
6. To the same wok, add garlic and ginger. Sauté for about 10 to 15 seconds then return beef to wok. Toss in heated broccoli. Slightly stir prepared sauce to make sure cornstarch is not settled on the bottom, then add to wok. Toss everything in sauce to combine. Continue cooking until sauce becomes thick.
7. Garnish with sesame seeds. Serve.

PF Chang's Mongolian Beef

Mongolian beef is an Asian restaurant favorite and this recipe inspired by PF Chang's is sure to please.

Serves 4–6 | Prep. time 15 minutes | Cooking time 10 minutes

Ingredients
1 cup vegetable oil
1½ pounds flank steak
½ cup cornstarch
¼ teaspoon red pepper flakes (optional)
1 bunch green onions, diagonal cut into 2-inch pieces
Rice for serving

Sauce

1 tablespoon vegetable oil
1–2 teaspoons ginger, minced
1 tablespoon garlic, minced
½ cup soy sauce
½ cup water
¾ cup dark brown sugar

Directions

1. Prepare the sauce by heating the oil in a medium saucepan over medium-high heat. Add the ginger and garlic. Stir and cook for about 30 seconds.
2. Add the soy sauce, water and brown sugar. Bring mixture to a boil, then reduce heat slightly and allow to simmer until the sauce begins to thicken.
3. Prepare steak by slicing it into ¼-inch slices, working against the grain to keep it tender. Place the cornstarch in a shallow dish, then dredge the sliced beef in the cornstarch to coat, shaking off any excess.
4. While the beef sits, heat the oil in a skillet over medium-high heat. When hot, add the beef and cook for about 3 minutes or until brown and crisp. Make sure to cook on both sides.
5. Remove the beef from the skillet and place on a plate. Drain the oil from the skillet and put the beef back in. Add the sauce and cook, stirring to make sure the beef is covered with sauce.
6. Sprinkle in the red pepper flakes and green onions.
7. Remove from heat and serve with rice.

PF Chang's Beef A La Sichuan

Another spicy recipe inspired by PF Chang's. This Beef A La Sichuan will surely warm you up on a cold night.

Serves 4–6 | Prep. time 20 minutes | Cooking time 10 minutes

Ingredients
Stir-fry
1 pound flank steak or sirloin, sliced thin
4 medium celery ribs
2 medium carrots
1 green onion
¼ cup peanut oil or canola oil
¼ cup cornstarch
½ teaspoon red pepper flakes
1½ teaspoons sesame oil

Sauce

3 tablespoons soy sauce
2 tablespoons hoisin sauce
1 tablespoon garlic and red chili paste
½ teaspoon Chinese hot mustard
1 teaspoon rice wine vinegar
½ teaspoon chili oil
2 teaspoons brown sugar
1 teaspoon garlic, minced
½ teaspoon fresh ginger, minced
½ teaspoon red pepper flakes

Directions
1. Whisk together all of the sauce ingredients in a mixing bowl. Set aside.
2. Slice the carrots and celery as thinly as possible and set aside.
3. Place the sliced beef in a medium bowl and sprinkle it with the cornstarch. Make sure every piece is coated. Allow to sit for 10 minutes.
4. Heat the oil in a large skillet or wok over medium-high heat and cook the beef until crispy, about 4–5 minutes. When done, remove beef from the oil to a paper-towel-lined plate to drain.
5. Discard any oil remaining in the skillet.
6. Add the sesame oil to the same skillet and heat over high heat. Add the celery, stir and cook for about 1 minute. Add the crushed red pepper and stir. Add the carrots, cooking and stirring for another 30 seconds.
7. Add the beef and green onions and stir, then pour the sauce into the skillet and bring to a boil. Allow to cook for 1 more minute, then serve over rice.

P.F. Chang's Beef and Broccoli

This healthy and tasty dish will satisfy more of your Asian cravings. With this recipe, you can make your favorite classic Asian dish in the comfort of your own home.

Serves 4 | Prep. time 45 minutes | Cooking time 15 minutes

Ingredients
Marinade
⅓ cup oyster sauce
2 teaspoons toasted sesame oil

⅓ cup sherry
1 teaspoon soy sauce
1 teaspoon white sugar
1 teaspoon corn starch

Beef and Broccoli
¾ pound beef round steak, cut into ⅛-inch thick strips
3 tablespoons vegetable oil
1 thin slice of fresh ginger root
1 clove garlic, peeled and smashed
1 pound broccoli, cut into florets

Preparation
1. Mix the marinade ingredients in a bowl until they have dissolved.
2. Marinate the beef in the mixture for 30 minutes.
3. Sauté the ginger and garlic in hot oil for a minute.
4. When the oil is flavored, remove the garlic and ginger and add in the broccoli. Continue cooking the broccoli until tender.
5. When the broccoli is cooked, transfer it to a bowl and set aside. Pour the beef and the marinade into the pan in which you cooked the broccoli and continue cooking until beef is cooked, or about 5 minutes.
6. Pour the broccoli back in and keep cooking for another 3 minutes.
7. Transfer to a bowl or plate and serve.

PF Chang's Pepper Steak

This recipe pays homage to PF Chang's pepper steak that is served in the restaurant.

Serves 4 | Prep. time 15 minutes | Cooking time 3 hours

Ingredients
1½ pounds beef sirloin
Garlic powder to taste
2½ tablespoons vegetable oil
1 cube or 1 teaspoon beef bouillon
¼ cup hot water
½ tablespoon cornstarch
⅓ cup onion, roughly chopped
1 green bell pepper, roughly chopped
1 red bell pepper, roughly chopped
2½ tablespoons soy sauce

1 teaspoon white sugar
½ teaspoon salt
½ teaspoon black pepper
½ cup water

Directions
1. Cut the beef into pieces approximately 1½ inches long and 1 inch wide.
2. Sprinkle the garlic powder over the beef and give it a quick stir.
3. Dissolve the bouillon in the hot water. Stir until the bouillon has completely dissolved, then stir in the cornstarch until that is completely mixed in as well.
4. Heat the oil in a large skillet or wok over medium-high heat. When hot, add the beef and vegetables. Cook just long enough to brown the beef, then transfer to a crock pot.
5. Stir the bouillon mixture a bit, then pour it over the beef in the slow cooker.
6. Add the onions, peppers, soy sauce, sugar, salt, and pepper. Add ½ cup water around the sides of the cooker.
7. Place the cover on the slow cooker and cook for about 3 hours on high or 6 hours on low.
8. Serve with rice.

P.F. Chang's Spare Ribs

Asian spare ribs are special—the flavor is undoubtedly one of a kind. Prepare this dish for your next meal if you are in an Oriental mood.

Serves 2 | Prep. time 5 minutes | Cooking time 25 minutes

Ingredients
Sauce
1 cup ketchup
1 cup light corn syrup
½ cup hoisin sauce
½ cup water
⅓ cup light brown sugar, packed
2 tablespoons onions, minced
1 tablespoon rice vinegar

Ribs
12 to 16 cups water
2 teaspoons salt
1 rack pork spareribs
4 cups vegetable oil
1 teaspoon sesame seeds, for garnish
1 tablespoon green onion, diced, for garnish

Preparation
1. Mix all of the sauce ingredients together and bring to a boil. When the sauce starts to boil, reduce it to a simmer for 5 minutes. Set aside.
2. Place the water and salt into a large pot or Dutch oven and bring to a boil. While the water is coming to a boil, clean the spare ribs, removing the excess fat.
3. When the water is boiling, place all the ribs into the water and continue boiling for 12 to 14 minutes.
4. Drain and set aside.
5. While the ribs are cooling, heat the oil to 375°F. Prepare a plate by covering it with a paper towel.
6. When the oil is hot enough, place 4 to 6 ribs in it and fry for 6 minutes.
7. Repeat step 6 until all the ribs are fried.
8. Mix the fried ribs and the sauce over medium heat. Simmer for at least a minute.
9. Transfer the ribs to a plate or bowl and serve with rice. Garnish the ribs with the sesame seeds and green onions.

PF Chang's Dan Dan Noodles

This recipe is a tribute to the flavorful Dan Dan Noodles you can get at PF Chang's.

Serves 4 | Prep. time 5 minutes | Cooking time 5 minutes

Ingredients
1 teaspoon oil
2 tablespoons green onion, minced
½ teaspoon garlic, minced
½ teaspoon chili paste
¼ pound ground pork or chicken, cooked
1 (14- ounce) package Asian egg noodles, cooked
1 teaspoon cornstarch
2 teaspoons water

Sauce

2 ounces soy sauce
1 ounce cooking wine
1 teaspoon oyster sauce
1 teaspoon granulated sugar
¾ cup chicken stock

Directions

1. Heat 1 teaspoon of oil in a large skillet or wok. When hot, add the chili paste, garlic and green onion and cook for 5–10 seconds.
2. Add the cooked chicken and stir for another 10 seconds. Add the soy sauce, wine, oyster sauce, sugar and chicken stock and cook for another 20 seconds.
3. Mix the cornstarch with 1 teaspoon of water to make a slurry. Stir into the sauce to thicken it. You can make more slurry if it isn't getting thick enough with the cornstarch and water.
4. Pour the sauce over the cooked egg noodles.
5. Serve garnished with bean sprouts and thinly sliced cucumber if desired.

Pei Wei's Beef Lo Mein

This beef lo mein recipe is a copycat version of the one on Pei Wei's menu.

Serves 4–6 | Prep. time 30 minutes | Cooking time 8 minutes

Ingredients
1½ pounds flank steak, cut into thin strips
1 tablespoon soy sauce
1½ teaspoons cornstarch
2 tablespoons oyster sauce
2 teaspoons dark soy sauce
¼ cup beef broth
1 teaspoon granulated sugar

½ pound fresh egg noodles or Italian spaghetti, cooked
1 teaspoon sesame oil
1 large carrot, julienned
½ cup Napa cabbage, chopped
1 clove garlic, chopped
1 quart of oil for stir-frying, or as needed
2-3 green onions, green parts only chopped, for garnish

Directions
1. Put the soy sauce and cornstarch in a resealable bag. Squish the bag to combine, then add the strips of steak and allow to marinate for 20 minutes.
2. In a mixing bowl, stir together the oyster sauce, dark soy sauce, beef broth and sugar. Set aside.
3. Toss the cooked noodles with 1 teaspoon of sesame oil and set aside.
4. Add the oil to a deep skillet and heat. When hot, add the beef, stirring constantly until the beef browns and begins to crisp.
5. Add 2 tablespoons of oil to a large skillet or wok and heat over medium-high heat. When hot, stir in the garlic and cook for about 30 seconds. Add the carrots and cook for another minute or so. Add the shredded cabbage and cook for another minute.
6. Stir in the noodles and cook for 2 minutes.
7. Add the sauce you prepared earlier to the skillet along with the beef. Stir to make sure everything is coated with sauce.
8. Garnish with green onions and serve.

Edo Japan's Sukiyaki Beef

Edo Japan may not be as popular as the other Asian restaurants, but their sukiyaki beef is delicious. This recipe is a take on the original that will just about make up for the fact that you can't find this amazing restaurant everywhere. Sukiyaki sauce, meanwhile, is usually found beside the soy sauce at the grocery store.

Serves 2–4 | Prep. time 15 min. | Marinating time 20 min. | Cooking time 5–6 min.

Ingredients
10 ounces sirloin steak, thinly sliced
½ carrot, thinly sliced
½ onion, sliced
1 green pepper, sliced
½ yellow bell pepper, sliced
½ cup sukiyaki sauce, divided

1 tablespoon oil
1 teaspoon chopped garlic
2 tablespoons ginger, finely chopped
2 teaspoons soy sauce
1 teaspoon sugar
1 tablespoon oyster sauce

Directions
1. Pour half of the sukiyaki sauce into a medium bowl and add the sliced beef. Let the beef marinate for 20 minutes.
2. Heat the oil in a large skillet. Add the garlic and cook for about 30 seconds.
3. Add the beef, with the sauce. Cook over medium-high heat until the beef is cooked through.
4. Add the ginger, carrots, peppers and onions and cook until the veggies have begun to soften.
5. Add the rest of the sukiyaki sauce along with the oyster sauce, soy sauce and sugar. Cook and stir for about 2 more minutes.
6. Serve over rice.

FISH & SEAFOOD

PF Chang's Shrimp Fried Rice

This recipe is another variation of traditional fried rice. PF Chang's shrimp fried rice inspired this recipe you can make at home.

Serves 4 | Prep. time 15 minutes | Cooking time 10 minutes

Ingredients
¼ teaspoon mustard, finely ground
¼ teaspoon ginger, minced
½ teaspoon garlic, minced or crushed
1 teaspoon molasses
1½ teaspoons soy sauce, plus some more to serve
2 tablespoons butter
2 eggs

Salt and pepper to taste
4 teaspoons canola oil
1½ packed cups tail-off large shrimp, cooked from frozen
¾ cup petite green peas, frozen or bean sprouts
¾ cup baby carrots, cut into matchsticks
2 cups steamed rice
3 green onions, chopped, use only white light green parts

Directions
1. In a small mixing bowl, whisk together the mustard, ginger, garlic and molasses. When those are combined, stir in the soy sauce. Set aside.
2. In a large skillet or wok, melt the butter over medium-high heat. Beat the eggs in a small dish with salt and pepper. When the skillet is hot, pour the eggs into it. Tilt the skillet to spread the eggs out like you are making an omelet. Brown the eggs on one side, then flip and cook for about 1 minute more.
3. Transfer to a plate and cut into small pieces.
4. Add more butter or oil to the pan and heat it over medium-high heat. Add the shrimp and cook for 1 minute. Add the carrots and peas and cook for about 2 minutes more or until the shrimp is hot throughout.
5. Add the steamed rice to the skillet and stir. Cook for a minute more, then pour the soy sauce mixture over the top and cook for another minute or two.
6. Remove from heat and stir in the green onions and egg.

PF Chang's Kung Pao Shrimp

This recipe for Kung Pao Shrimp is based on the super flavorful dish offered on PF Chang's menu.

Serves 4 | Prep. time 10 minutes | Cooking time 10 minutes

Ingredients
¼ cup soy sauce
½ teaspoon cornstarch
2 tablespoons water

¼ teaspoon sesame oil
½ teaspoon balsamic vinegar
½ teaspoon sugar
Pepper to taste
3 tablespoons hot chili oil
3 cloves garlic, minced
¼ onion, roughly chopped
16 large shrimp, peeled and deveined
¼ cup roasted peanuts
5 scallions, chopped

Directions

1. In a mixing bowl, whisk together the soy sauce, cornstarch, water, sesame oil, balsamic vinegar, sugar and pepper. Set aside.
2. Add the hot chili oil to a deep skillet or wok and heat over medium-high heat.
3. Add the minced garlic and onion and cook for about 2 minutes. If you want to add other vegetables, like broccoli or peas, you can add them now.
4. Cook until the veggies are soft. Add the shrimp and cook for about 2 minutes, then stir in the sauce you made earlier and cook a bit longer until the sauce thickens. Stir to coat the shrimp, then remove the skillet from the heat and stir in the scallions and peanuts.
5. Serve with rice.

PF Chang's Crispy Honey Shrimp

These crispy shrimp are delicious when you make this copycat recipe of the menu item found at PF Chang's.

Serves 2 | Prep. time 15 minutes | Cooking time 5 minutes

Ingredients
½ pound shrimp, peeled and deveined

Batter
1 cup all-purpose flour
½ cup cornstarch
¼ teaspoon baking powder
1 egg
1 cup ice water

Shrimp marinade
1 tablespoon low-sodium soy sauce
1½ tablespoons cornstarch
Pinch of salt
Pinch of black pepper
1 cup vegetable oil for frying

Honey sauce
½ cup rice wine
⅓ cup honey
⅓ cup rice vinegar
3 tablespoons low-sodium soy sauce
1 tablespoon garlic, minced
¼ cup corn starch
¼ cup water

Garnish
Green onions, chopped

Directions
1. Clean the shrimp, pat them dry, and add them to a bowl.
2. Season the shrimp with some salt and pepper, then mix in the cornstarch and stir to ensure all of the shrimp are evenly covered. Stir in the soy sauce, then cover and refrigerate for about 10 minutes.
3. To make the batter, mix together the flour, baking powder, egg, iced water, and cornstarch in a large bowl. Stir with a fork to ensure it is well combined. Put the batter in the refrigerator until you are ready to use it.
4. In a heavy saucepan, heat the vegetable oil to 350°F.
5. Dip the shrimp in the batter one at a time, shaking them a bit to remove extra batter.
6. Drop the battered shrimp into the hot oil and cook until golden brown and crispy.

7. Transfer the shrimp from the oil to a paper-towel-lined plate to drain.
8. In a small cup or bowl, stir cornstarch into the water to make a slurry.
9. In a saucepan, whisk together the wine, honey, vinegar, soy sauce and garlic. Bring to a boil over medium-high heat, then reduce heat to low and whisk in the cornstarch slurry a little at a time until the sauce thickens to the desired honey-like consistency.
10. Add the shrimp to a serving bowl and pour the sauce over the top. Stir carefully to combine.
11. Garnish with green onions and serve.

VEGETARIAN AND SIDE DISHES

Panda Express's Chow Mein

Sometimes, all you want is some delicious chow mein. This recipe is inspired by the super tasty chow mein you find at Panda Express. Yaki Soba noodles are found in the produce section of the grocery store; usually the three small packages you'll need are sold together in one 17-ounce pack.

Serves 4 | Prep. time 10 minutes | Cooking time 5 minutes

Ingredients
¼ cup soy sauce
1 tablespoon brown sugar
2 cloves garlic, minced
1 teaspoon fresh ginger, grated
Ground black pepper to taste

2–3 tablespoons vegetable oil
3 (5.6-ounce) packages refrigerated Yaki Soba noodles
⅔ cup celery, chopped diagonally
1 medium onion, thinly sliced
2 cups cabbage, chopped

Directions
1. In a mixing bowl, stir together the soy sauce, brown sugar, garlic, ginger and pepper.
2. Rinse the Yaki Soba noodles well, then drain.
3. In a large skillet or wok, heat the oil over medium-high heat. When hot, add the celery and onions and cook for about 2 minutes.
4. Add the cabbage to the skillet and cook for another minute or so, until it starts to soften.
5. Stir in the Yaki Soba noodles and soy sauce mixture and cook for another 3 minutes.

PF Chang's Spicy Green Beans

PF Chang's Spicy Green Beans are a must-order side dish when visiting the restaurant. This recipe is a take on what you will find in the restaurant.

Serves 4–6 | Prep. time 5 minutes | Cooking time 5 minutes

Ingredients
1–2 pounds green beans, trimmed and cut into 2-inch pieces
2 green onions, thinly chopped
½ -1 teaspoon red pepper flakes, more if you like it spicier

4 cloves garlic, minced
2 tablespoons sesame oil
⅛ teaspoon salt
⅛ teaspoon ground black pepper
2 tablespoons low-sodium soy sauce
1 tablespoon rice vinegar
1 teaspoon white granulated sugar
¼ cup water
1 teaspoon cornstarch

Directions
1. In a mixing bowl, stir together the soy sauce, rice vinegar, sugar, water, cornstarch, salt and pepper. Set aside.
2. In a large skillet or wok, heat the sesame oil over medium-high heat. After 30 seconds, add the garlic, green onions and 1 teaspoon of red pepper flakes. Cook and stir for about 30 seconds.
3. After 30 seconds, add the green beans. Stir constantly until they are cooked through, then push them to the side of the pan. Pour the sauce you made earlier into the other side, stirring as you pour. Cook until the sauce boils, then stir the beans into the sauce, making sure they are all covered. Cook for another 30 seconds.

PF Chang's Garlic Noodles

This garlic noodles recipe is a take on what you will find at PF Chang's. A perfect accompaniment to any meal.

Serves 4 | Prep. time 5 minutes | Cooking time 5 minutes

Ingredients
1 pound fresh Chinese noodles or vermicelli, cooked tender and rinsed in cool water
3 teaspoons garlic, minced
3 teaspoons sugar
2 teaspoons white vinegar
1½ teaspoons red chili flakes*
2 teaspoons canola oil

½ teaspoon sesame oil
2 teaspoons chopped cilantro
1 English cucumber, seeds removed and julienned, for garnish

Sauce
¾ cup water
1 teaspoon chicken base powder
1 teaspoon sugar
2 teaspoons Chinese shao hsing wine
1 teaspoon oyster sauce
½ teaspoon salt
1 teaspoon cornstarch

Directions
1. Place the cooled, cooked noodles in a mixing bowl. Add the red chili flakes, sesame oil and cilantro and toss to combine.
2. Add the oil to a large skillet or wok and heat over medium-high heat. When hot, add the garlic and cook for about 30 seconds, then add the sugar and vinegar.
3. In a mixing bowl, mix together all the sauce ingredients, stirring until it thickens a bit.
4. Add the noodles to the skillet and pour in the sauce, stirring until the noodles are hot and covered with the sauce.
5. Serve with sliced cucumber on the side.

* you can adjust the spiciness to suit your taste with more or less chili pepper flakes

PF Chang's Shanghai Cucumbers

This recipe is a flavorful take on PF Chang's Shanghai cucumbers.

Serves 4 | Prep. time 5 minutes | Cooking time

Ingredients
2 English cucumbers, peeled and chopped
3 tablespoons soy sauce
½ teaspoon sesame oil
1 teaspoon white vinegar
Sprinkle of toasted sesame seeds

Directions
1. Stir together the soy sauce, sesame oil and vinegar in a serving dish.
2. Add the cucumbers and toss to coat.
3. Sprinkle with the sesame seeds.

California Pizza Kitchen's
Kung Pao Spaghetti

You may not think of CPK as an Asian restaurant, but their Kung Pao Spaghetti is legendary. This recipe pays tribute to the restaurant's version and allows you to make it at home.

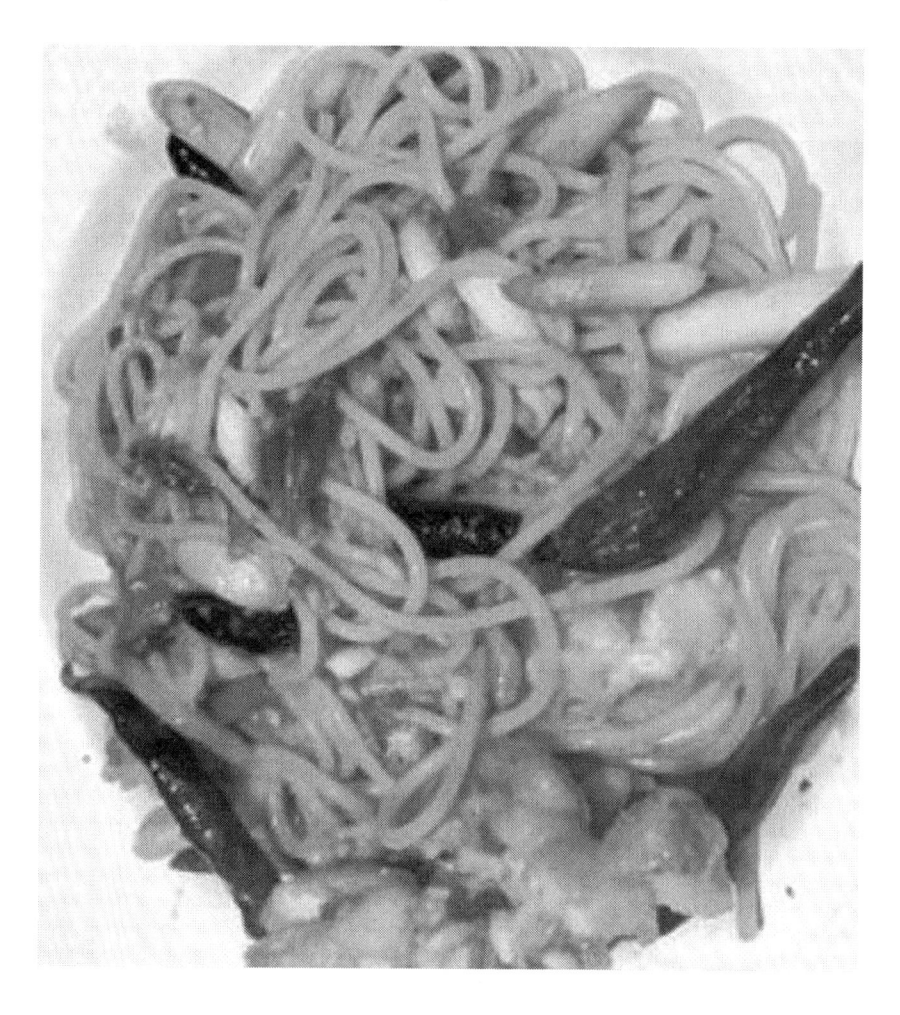

Serves 4–6 | Prep. Time 10 minutes | Cooking time 10 minutes

Ingredients

1 cup chicken stock
4 tablespoons cornstarch, divided
¾ cup soy sauce
½ cup sherry
3 tablespoons chili paste with garlic
¼ cup sugar
2 tablespoons red wine vinegar
2 tablespoons sesame oil
2 egg whites
½ teaspoon salt
1 pound spaghetti
¼ cup olive oil
1 pound boneless skinless chicken breast, cut into ¾-inch cubes
10–15 whole Chinese dried red chili peppers; DO NOT eat these, they are for color and heat!
1 cup unsalted dry roasted peanuts
¼ cup garlic, minced
3 cups green onions, greens and white parts, coarsely chopped

Directions

1. Make the sauce by whisking together the chicken stock and 2 tablespoons of cornstarch. Stir until the cornstarch dissolves.
2. Whisk in the soy sauce, sherry, chili paste, sugar, vinegar and sesame oil. Bring to a boil.
3. Turn the heat down and simmer until the sauce thickens, about 20 minutes.
4. In a small mixing bowl, whisk together the egg whites, 2 tablespoons of cornstarch and salt. Stir until well blended, but not so much that the egg whites froth.
5. Bring salted water to a fast boil in a large pot. Add the pasta and cook until not quite al dente. Drain.
6. Heat the olive oil in a large skillet over medium-high heat.

7. Add the cut chicken pieces to the egg white mixture and stir to coat. Carefully add the chicken and egg white mixture to the skillet to form a "pancake".
8. Cook until the egg sets, then flip and cook on the other side. Separate the chicken pieces.
9. When the chicken pieces turn golden brown, stir in the garlic and scallions and allow to cook for about 30 seconds. Add the sauce that you made earlier and stir to make sure it covers everything. Add the pasta and stir to combine with the sauce.
10. Mix in the peppers and peanuts.
11. Serve with scallions.

Pei Wei's Teriyaki Sauce

This recipe pays tribute to the amazing teriyaki sauce at Pei Wei. Once you have the sauce down, the possibilities are endless.

Yield about 2 cups | Prep. time 5 minutes | Cooking time 7 minutes

Ingredients

1 cup soy sauce
½ cup water
1 teaspoon ginger, freshly grated
½ teaspoon granulated garlic
⅓ cup brown sugar
1 tablespoon molasses
1 tablespoon orange zest, grated
2 tablespoons cornstarch
¼ cup water

Directions

1. In a saucepan, stir together the soy sauce, water, garlic, ginger, brown sugar, molasses and orange zest.
2. Bring the mixture to a boil over medium-high heat.
3. Make a slurry with the cornstarch and water.
4. When the soy sauce mixture boils, whisk in the cornstarch slurry and reduce the heat to medium.
5. Let the sauce simmer for about 5 minutes, whisking the whole time, until it thickens. Remove it from the heat and let it stand. It will continue to thicken as it sits. You can add more water if it gets too thick.
6. Use with any of your favorite teriyaki recipes.

Pei Wei's Fried Rice

This fried rice recipe is a close copy of what they serve at Pei Wei.

Serves 4 | Prep. time 5 minutes | Cooking time 5 minutes

Ingredients
2 cups enriched white rice, cooked
1 quart water
⅔ cup chopped baby carrots, cooked
½ cup bean sprouts

2 tablespoons vegetable oil
2 eggs
Soy sauce to taste
Sesame oil to taste

Directions
1. Heat a large skillet or wok over medium-high heat, then add the vegetable oil.
2. Add the cooked carrots and bean sprouts and cook for 30 seconds.
3. Crack the eggs into the skillet and stir to scramble them with the vegetables.
4. After the eggs are cooked, stir in the cooked rice. Add soy sauce and sesame oil to taste.

Pei Wei's Soba Miso Bowl

This recipe, which is inspired by Pei Wei's Soba Miso Bowl, is a great dish for a cool night.

Serves 4 | Prep. time 10 minutes | Cooking time 15 minutes

Ingredients
6 ounces chicken, sliced
¼ pound shrimp
3 ounces firm tofu
2 tablespoons miso paste
Salt and white pepper to taste
1 tablespoon ginger, minced
1 tablespoon white scallion, sliced
2 tablespoons black mushroom, sliced
2 ounces Napa cabbage, thinly sliced
¼ pound washed spinach leaves
Chicken stock or water as needed
1 tablespoon garlic, minced
1 cup Miso Sauce (see recipe below)
22 ounces Soba noodles, cooked
1 teaspoon sesame oil

Miso Sauce
1 cup miso paste
2 cups mirin
½ cup sake
2 tablespoons lemon juice

Directions
1. Prepare the miso sauce by whisking together the ingredients. Cover and refrigerate.
2. Season the shrimp, chicken and tofu with miso paste, salt and pepper. Cover and marinate for 1 hour.
3. Heat a large skillet or wok over medium-high heat. Add the water or chicken stock and bring to a simmer. Add the seasoned chicken, shrimp and tofu and stir-fry for about 1 minute.
4. Add the miso sauce and stir to cover the chicken, shrimp and tofu.
5. Add the cooked noodles to the skillet and turn down the heat. Stir for about 30 seconds to heat the noodles, then add the spinach leaves. Stir until the spinach begins to wilt.
6. Drizzle in the sesame oil and serve.

DESSERTS

P.F. Chang's Coconut Pineapple Ice Cream with Banana Spring Rolls

The perfect combination of cold, creamy tropical-flavored ice cream with crispy banana-filled spring rolls.

Serves 6 | Prep. Time 5 minutes | Cooking time 30 minutes

Ingredients
Ice cream
1 (13½-ounce) can coconut milk
1 cup granulated sugar
1½ cups heavy cream
1 teaspoon coconut extract
1 (8-ounce) can crushed pineapple, drained
⅓ cup shredded coconut

Banana spring rolls
3 ripe bananas, preferably plantains, halved horizontally
3 rice paper or wonton wrappers
1–3 tablespoons brown sugar
1 teaspoon cinnamon
Oil, for frying
Caramel sauce, for drizzling (optional)

Paste for sealing wrappers
2 tablespoons water
2 teaspoons flour or cornstarch

Preparation
1. Make the ice cream. Place coconut milk and sugar in a mixing bowl. Mix with electric mixer until sugar is dissolved. Mix in remaining ingredients until well-blended. Place in ice cream maker to churn and follow manufacturer's instructions until ice cream holds when scooped with a spoon, about 30 minutes. Transfer to a container with lid and freeze for at least 2 hours or until desired firmness is reached.
2. Make the banana spring rolls. Lay wrapper on a flat surface. Position a banana slice near the edge of the wrapper closest to you, at the bottom. Sprinkle with about 1 teaspoon to 1 tablespoon brown sugar, depending how sweet you want it. Sprinkle with a pinch or two of cinnamon. Roll up like a burrito, tucking in the sides. In a small bowl, stir the paste ingredients together. Brush the paste on the edge of the wrapper and seal the roll. Place roll, sealed side down, on a plate and repeat with the remaining bananas. Heat oil, about 1–1½ inches deep, over medium to high heat. Fry the rolls until golden brown, about 1–2 minutes on each side. Place on paper towels to drain.
3. Serve the rolls with scoops of ice cream and drizzle with caramel sauce, if desired.

Chinese Restaurants' Banana Wontons

Little pockets of banana goodness. This recipe is the perfect ending to a meal.

Makes 12 | Prep. time 5 minutes | Cooking time 3 minutes

Ingredients
2-3 diced bananas
2 tablespoons walnuts, chopped
1 tablespoon brown sugar
¼ teaspoon ground cinnamon
¼ teaspoon nutmeg
Pinch of salt
12 wonton wrappers
Frying oil
Honey or chocolate sauce for drizzle
Sesame seed for garnish
Ice cream for serving

Directions
1. In a small bowl, combine the bananas, nuts, spices and salt.
2. Separate the wonton wrappers and place about a tablespoon of the mixture onto the center of each. Don't overfill, because you need to seal the wrappers tightly.
3. Use your finger or a pastry brush to spread a bit of water around the edges of the wrappers. Fold them into triangles, pinching the edges to seal.
4. Pour enough oil into a large skillet so that the wrappers will float and not touch the bottom.
5. Cook in batches until golden brown, about 1½ minutes on each side.
6. Drizzle with honey or chocolate sauce and a sprinkle of sesame seeds. Serve with ice cream if desired.

P.F. Chang's Ginger Panna Cotta

If you need to clean your palate after a heavy meal, here is a dessert that will refresh your taste buds. Thank you, P.F. Chang, for this wonderful treat.

Serves 3 | Prep. Time 10 minutes | Cooking time 4 hours 10 minutes

Ingredients

Panna cotta
¼ cup heavy cream
½ cup granulated sugar
1 tablespoon grated ginger
1½ tablespoons powdered gelatin
6 tablespoons warm water

Strawberry sauce
2 pounds ripe strawberries, hulled
½ cup granulated sugar
2 teaspoons cornstarch
½ lemon, juice
1 pinch salt

Preparation
1. Place the cream, sugar and ginger in a saucepan and cook over medium-low heat, until the sugar dissolves. Remove the mixture from heat and set aside.
2. In a medium-sized bowl, mix the water and the gelatin together. Set aside for a few minutes.
3. After the gelatin has rested, pour the sugar mixture into the medium-sized bowl and stir, removing all lumps.
4. Grease your ramekins and then transfer the mixture into the ramekins, leaving 2 inches of space at the top.
5. Place the ramekins in your refrigerator or freezer to let them set for *at least* 4 hours.
6. While the panna cottas are setting, make the strawberry sauce by cooking all the sauce ingredients in a medium-sized pan for 10 minutes. Stir the mixture occasionally, then remove from heat.
7. When the panna cottas are ready, flip over the containers onto a plate and allow the gelatin to stand. Drizzle with the strawberry sauce and serve.

Easy Chinese Restaurants' Doughnuts

These wonderful little donuts are just like the ones you can find in a Chinese restaurant.

Serves 4 | Prep. time 2 minutes | Cooking time 5 minutes

Ingredients

1 can refrigerator biscuits, such as crescent rolls
Sugar for coating
Cinnamon for coating
2 cups vegetable oil

Directions
1. Cut the biscuits into small pieces.
2. Heat the vegetable oil in a medium saucepan.
3. Carefully drop the biscuit pieces into the hot oil and cook until they turn golden brown. It should only take a couple of minutes. The dough will also float to the top when ready.
4. Remove and drain on a paper-towel-lined plate.
5. Combine the sugar and cinnamon in a shallow dish. Roll the finished donuts in the mixture to coat.

Twin Dragon's Almond Cookies

An Asian dinner is hardly complete without almond cookies. This recipe lets you make these wonderful cookies at home.

Makes 24 | Prep. time 10 minutes | Cooking time 20 minutes

Ingredients
3 cups flour
1 teaspoon baking soda
½ teaspoon salt
1 cup blanched almonds
1 cup granulated sugar
1½ cups lard
1 teaspoon almond extract
1 large egg, beaten
2 tablespoons water

Directions
1. Preheat oven to 350°F.
2. In a mixing bowl, combine the flour, baking soda and salt.
3. Grind the blanched almonds to a powder and add them to the flour mixture.
4. In a different mixing bowl, cream together the sugar, lard, almond extract, egg and water.
5. Add the flour mixture and mix until everything is well combined.
6. Use an ungreased cookie sheet to bake the cookies. Form the dough into balls and place them far enough apart that they don't touch each other and have room to spread.
7. Press an almond into the center of each cookie, then brush with beaten egg.
8. Bake for 20 minutes or until the edges start to turn a light brown.

Takeout Fortune Cookies

Who doesn't love fortune cookies? They are sweet, crisp, and can predict your future! They are easy to make at home and best of all you write the fortune message.

Serves 36 | Prep. Time 15 minutes | Cooking time 10 minutes

Ingredients
3 egg whites
¾ cup white sugar
½ cup butter, melted and cooled
¼ teaspoon vanilla extract
¼ teaspoon almond extract
1 cup all-purpose flour
2 tablespoons water

Directions
1. Prepare fortunes on strips of paper.
2. Preheat the oven to 375°F.
3. Line cookie sheets with parchment paper, or spray with non-stick spray.
4. Using an electric mixer, whip the egg whites and sugar at high speed until frothy, about 2 minutes.
5. Reduce the mixer speed to low, and mix in the melted butter, vanilla, almond extract, flour, and water.
6. Spoon the batter onto the cookie sheets in 3-inch circles. Repeat until the batter is used up. Be sure to leave enough space between circles.
7. Bake until the edges begin to turn golden brown, 5-7 minutes. Do not overbake, or they will be too stiff to fold. If you under-bake them, their texture will be too spongy.
8. Quickly take a circle, put the fortune strip on the center, and fold the cookie in half over the fortune.
9. Fold the ends together to make a horseshoe shape.
10. Allow to cool and set. You may put them in muffin pans to prevent them from springing open.

RECIPE INDEX

APPETIZERS _____ 3
  Panda Express's Chicken Potstickers _____ 3
  Panda Express's Cream Cheese Rangoon _____ 5
  Panda Express's Chicken Egg Roll _____ 7
  Panda Express's Veggie Spring Roll _____ 9
  PF Chang's Hot and Sour Soup _____ 11
  PF Chang's Lettuce Wraps _____ 13
  PF Chang's Shrimp Dumplings _____ 15
  PF Chang's Spicy Chicken Noodle Soup _____ 17
  Takeout Dry Garlic Ribs _____ 19
  Pei Wei's Thai Chicken Satay _____ 21
  Pei Wei's Vietnamese Chicken Salad Spring Roll _____ 23
  Pei Wei's Crab Wonton _____ 25

CHICKEN _____ 27
  Panda Express's Grilled Teriyaki Chicken _____ 27
  Panda Express's Sweetfire Chicken Breast _____ 29
  Panda Express's Black Pepper Chicken _____ 31
  Panda Express's Zucchini Mushroom Chicken _____ 33
  Panda Express's Orange Chicken _____ 35
  PF Chang's Orange Peel Chicken _____ 37
  PF Chang's Chicken Fried Rice _____ 39
  PF Chang's Ginger Chicken with Broccoli _____ 41
  P.F. Chang's Crispy Honey Chicken _____ 43
  Pei Wei's Sesame Chicken _____ 46
  Pei Wei's Spicy Chicken _____ 49
  Pei Wei's Chicken Pad Thai _____ 51
  Pei Wei's Kung Pao Chicken _____ 53
  Pei Wei's Chicken Lo Mein _____ 55
  Pei Wei's Thai Blazing Noodles with Chicken _____ 57
  Pei Wei's Honey Seared Chicken _____ 59
  Pei Wei's Coconut Curry with Chicken _____ 61
  Pei Wei's Chopped Chicken Salad _____ 63

Pei Wei's Asian Diner Caramel Chicken	65
BEEF AND PORK	69
Panda Express's Beijing Beef	69
Panda Express's Copycat Beef and Broccoli	71
PF Chang's Mongolian Beef	73
PF Chang's Beef A La Sichuan	75
P.F. Chang's Beef and Broccoli	77
PF Chang's Pepper Steak	79
P.F. Chang's Spare Ribs	81
PF Chang's Dan Dan Noodles	83
Pei Wei's Beef Lo Mein	85
Edo Japan's Sukiyaki Beef	87
FISH & SEAFOOD	89
PF Chang's Shrimp Fried Rice	89
PF Chang's Kung Pao Shrimp	91
PF Chang's Crispy Honey Shrimp	93
VEGETARIAN AND SIDE DISHES	97
Panda Express's Chow Mein	97
PF Chang's Spicy Green Beans	99
PF Chang's Garlic Noodles	101
PF Chang's Shanghai Cucumbers	103
California Pizza Kitchen's Kung Pao Spaghetti	104
Pei Wei's Teriyaki Sauce	107
Pei Wei's Fried Rice	109
Pei Wei's Soba Miso Bowl	111
DESSERTS	113
P.F. Chang's Coconut Pineapple Ice Cream with Banana Spring Rolls	113
Chinese Restaurants' Banana Wontons	115
P.F. Chang's Ginger Panna Cotta	117
Easy Chinese Restaurants' Doughnuts	119
Twin Dragon's Almond Cookies	121
Takeout Fortune Cookies	123

ALSO BY LINA CHANG

CHINESE TAKEOUT COOKBOOK
Favorite Chinese Takeout Recipes to Make at Home
LINA CHANG

ITALIAN TAKEOUT COOKBOOK
Easy Italian Recipes to Make at Home Including Pizza and Pasta
LINA CHANG

THAI TAKEOUT COOKBOOK
Favorite Thai Food Takeout Recipes to Make at Home
LINA CHANG

GREEK TAKEOUT COOKBOOK
Favorite Greek Takeout Recipes to Make at Home
LINA CHANG

Indian TAKEOUT COOKBOOK
Favorite Indian Food Takeout Recipes to Make at Home
LINA CHANG

JAPANESE TAKEOUT COOKBOOK
Favorite Japanese Takeout Recipes to Make at Home
Sushi, Noodles, Rices, Salads, Miso Soups, Tempura, Teriyaki, and More
LINA CHANG

TEX-MEX TAKEOUT COOKBOOK
Favorite Tex-Mex Recipes to Make at Home
LINA CHANG

LEBANESE TAKEOUT COOKBOOK
Favorite Lebanese Takeout Recipes to Make at Home
LINA CHANG

KOREAN TAKEOUT COOKBOOK
Favorite Korean Takeout Recipes to Make at Home
LINA CHANG

APPENDIX

Cooking Conversion Charts

1. Measuring Equivalent Chart

Type	Imperial	Imperial	Metric
Weight	1 dry ounce		28g
	1 pound	16 dry ounces	0.45 kg
Volume	1 teaspoon		5 ml
	1 dessert spoon	2 teaspoons	10 ml
	1 tablespoon	3 teaspoons	15 ml
	1 Australian tablespoon	4 teaspoons	20 ml
	1 fluid ounce	2 tablespoons	30 ml
	1 cup	16 tablespoons	240 ml
	1 cup	8 fluid ounces	240 ml
	1 pint	2 cups	470 ml
	1 quart	2 pints	0.95 l
	1 gallon	4 quarts	3.8 l
Length	1 inch		2.54 cm

* Numbers are rounded to the closest equivalent

2. Oven Temperature Equivalent Chart

Fahrenheit (°F)	Celsius (°C)	Gas Mark
220	100	
225	110	1/4
250	120	1/2
275	140	1
300	150	2
325	160	3
350	180	4
375	190	5
400	200	6
425	220	7
450	230	8
475	250	9
500	260	

* Celsius (°C) = T (°F)-32] * 5/9
** Fahrenheit (°F) = T (°C) * 9/5 + 32
*** Numbers are rounded to the closest equivalent

Made in the USA
Columbia, SC
19 August 2021